POEMS A~~ND PRAYERS~~

for

AUTUMN

by
Mary
Fleeson

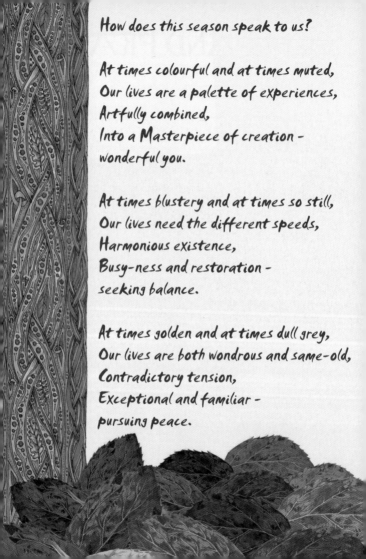

How does this season speak to us?

At times colourful and at times muted,
Our lives are a palette of experiences,
Artfully combined,
Into a Masterpiece of creation -
wonderful you.

At times blustery and at times so still,
Our lives need the different speeds,
Harmonious existence,
Busy-ness and restoration -
seeking balance.

At times golden and at times dull grey,
Our lives are both wondrous and same-old,
Contradictory tension,
Exceptional and familiar -
pursuing peace.

SEE HOW THE FARMER WAITS FOR THE LAND TO YIELD ITS VALUABLE CROP, PATIENTLY WAITING FOR THE AUTUMN AND SPRING RAINS. James 5:7

This is a time to remember,
And as the earth holds warmth within
Let good thoughts be held in my heart.

This is a time to thank,
And as the earth gives us food
Let gratitude be held in my heart.

This is a time to prepare,
And as the earth lies fallow awhile
Let divine peace be held in my heart.

LET US NOT BECOME WEARY IN DOING GOOD, FOR AT THE PROPER TIME WE WILL REAP A HARVEST IF WE DO NOT GIVE UP. Galatians 6:9

Someone once told me that sowing seeds
was what 'it' was about.
Planting ideas in fertile minds,
of love and forgiveness and hope.

Someone once told me that our Creator God
would water and nurture the ideas.
Those delicate idea seeds,
of love and forgiveness and hope.

Without You Lord, my love is like the turning tide,
fickle and changing,
but if I love because of my faith in You
and help others to love, then that love refreshes,
and You are glorified.

Without You Lord, my forgiveness is like the wind,
fleeting and ephemeral,
but if I forgive because of my faith
and help others to forgive, then that forgiveness releases,
and You are glorified.

Without You Lord, my hope is like the falling leaf,
fragile and dry,
but if I hope because of my faith
and help others to hope, then that hope renews,
and You are glorified.

THOUGH THE FIG TREE DOES NOT BUD AND THERE ARE NO GRAPES ON THE VINES, THOUGH THE OLIVE CROP FAILS AND THE FIELDS PRODUCE NO FOOD, THOUGH THERE ARE NO SHEEP IN THE PEN AND NO CATTLE IN THE STALLS, YET I WILL REJOICE IN THE LORD, I WILL BE JOYFUL IN GOD MY SAVIOUR. Habakkuk 3:17-18

When I have little,
Grant me enough,
When I have plenty,
Help me to share.

When I am fearful,
Grant me light,
When I am bold,
Help me to be wise.

When I am sad,
Grant me joy,
When I am content,
Help me to comfort.

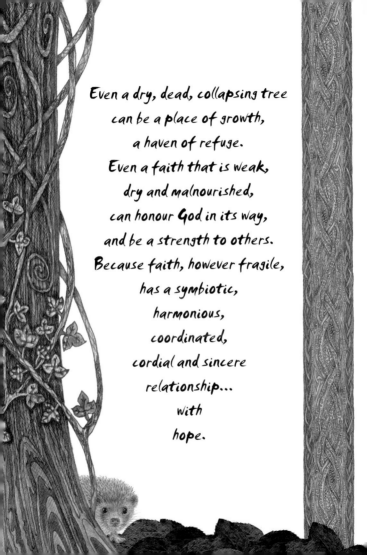

Even a dry, dead, collapsing tree
can be a place of growth,
a haven of refuge.
Even a faith that is weak,
dry and malnourished,
can honour God in its way,
and be a strength to others.
Because faith, however fragile,
has a symbiotic,
harmonious,
coordinated,
cordial and sincere
relationship...
with
hope.

AND GOODNESS IS THE HARVEST
THAT IS PRODUCED FROM
THE SEEDS THE PEACEMAKERS
PLANT IN PEACE. James 3:18

As the movement of the sea
On this cold morning,
Is balm to my fevered mind,
Let Your peace soothe my soul.

As the lap of a gentle wave
On the empty shore,
Helps me to breathe again
Let Your Spirit infuse me.

As the land prepares to rest
After a fruitful season,
Reminds me of my needs
Let Your wisdom guide me.

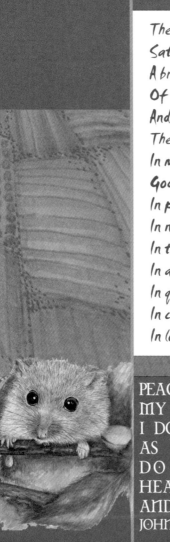

The world gave me a sort-of
Satisfaction,
A brief passionate fling
Of immediate needs met
And wishes granted.
Then I found,
In many guises and places,
God,
In people,
In nature,
In the sea and the land,
In art and music,
In quiet and in joyous noise,
In conversation and silence,
In love and in peace.

PEACE I LEAVE WITH YOU;
MY PEACE I GIVE YOU.
I DO NOT GIVE TO YOU
AS THE WORLD GIVES.
DO NOT LET YOUR
HEARTS BE TROUBLED
AND DO NOT BE AFRAID.
JOHN 14:27

SAY NOT YE, THERE ARE YET FOUR
MONTHS, AND THEN COMETH
HARVEST? BEHOLD, I SAY UNTO YOU,
LIFT UP YOUR EYES, AND LOOK ON
THE FIELDS; FOR THEY ARE WHITE
ALREADY TO HARVEST. John 4:35

No need to wait
for seasonal changes
to ripen the souls
of God's precious people,
simply tell what He did.

The Gospel is immediate.
Infinite power,
truth incarnate,
transforming agent,
simply tell what He said.

A word of wisdom,
a sentence inspired,
can speak
spirit to spirit.
simply tell your story.

THEREFORE SAID HE UNTO
THEM, THE HARVEST TRULY
IS GREAT, BUT THE
LABOURERS ARE FEW:
PRAY YE THEREFORE THE
LORD OF THE HARVEST,
THAT HE WOULD SEND
FORTH LABOURERS INTO
HIS HARVEST. Luke 10:2

He often spoke in stories,
Familiar scenes in familiar places,
Well-known ideas and well-known faces.
But what means the harvest to a city dweller?
Or the sea fishing boat to landlocked folk?
Today, to explain, tell your story,
How Your God saved you.
How God loves us.
How love is.

The raucous caw of blackest crows,
Misty skies and soft golden light,
Freshly-dug soil smelling,
and bonfire smoking.

Crisp fallen leaves crunching underfoot,
Shorter days and warmer clothes,
Sense of things ending,
and just beginning.

The precious harvest is in for now,
So rest and take stock,
The earth is preparing,
and Christ is coming.

Circle me, Creator God,
Keep peace within my mind,
Keep fear without.
Circle me, Loving God,
Keep joy within my heart,
Keep melancholy without.
Circle me, Saviour God,
Keep light within my spirit,
Keep darkness without.